The first version of this book was written as a letter to my dear friend David when he was about to become a dad. Davey, this book is for you and your family with all my love. Knowing you would be reading it, with your sweetness, humbleness and absurdity, made it easy for me to say clearly what I wanted to say.

YOU'LL BE A WONDERFUL DAD

ADVICE on BECOMING the BEST FATHER YOU CAN BE

AILSA WILD

with illustrations by BERNARD CALEO

Hardie Grant

BOOKS

Lots of this book talks to dads with female partners but I'm hoping there are elements here for all parents. If you're starting a rainbow family, Jasper Peach's book *You'll Be a Wonderful Parent: Advice and Encouragement for Rainbow Families of All Kinds* was written alongside this one and is for you especially.

CONTENTS

To begin

First up, I'm so excited you're going to be a dad. It makes me want to cry a little just thinking of all the big tender, precious love you're going to have.

Second, anyone who gives you advice about parenthood is probably talking to their past self or partner and not to you at all.

So, keeping that in mind, here's a big old dollop of advice as you begin this parenting adventure.

I want to start with this: the current of sexism is stronger when you're a parent, and it's hard to swim against. If you're in a male-female relationship (as I am), you're much more likely to get caught in traditional gender roles once there's a babe.

Women, when they become mothers, are generally told what they must and mustn't do (far too frequently, by far too many people) and expectations of them are absurdly high. Many cultures hold lower expectations of men's capacity to parent, although that has been slowly changing.

As part of that change, this book is a collection of high expectations for you as a dad. It is a book about how to love your family in the face of a culture that has historically left women alone with the domestic work and held men separate from the warm hearts of their families.

I hope you don't feel like it's a list of difficult jobs. Sometimes these things might feel hard, but the work itself can often bring great joy and satisfaction. You'll try, you'll manage some things and not others, you'll make mistakes and learn as you go, and the love that grows will be rich and real.

This book goes through some of the practical and emotional aspects of being a great dad, which, in many ways, means being a great partner. **YOU'RE PARENTING TOGETHER AND THAT MEANS SUPPORTING EACH OTHER. YOU WILL NEED TO BACK EACH OTHER UP WITH YOUR HANDS, MINDS AND HEARTS.**

Some of what I'm going to tell you you'll already know (sorry for the bits where I state the obvious) and some of it may not be true of your unique situation. Your partner knows better than I do what she needs. Listen to her before you listen to me.

THIS TIME, OF BRINGING A BABY INTO THE WORLD, CAN BE A JUMBLE OF ANXIETY AND ANTICIPATION, AS WELL AS JOY. It may all seem unreal.

People might expect you to have feelings you don't have – but this time is not about them. Pay attention to your feelings for your own sake. Sit with them for a moment.

How are you? What is it like knowing there's a baby coming?

Take all the time you can to be with your partner and share your big love with her. You're doing something immense together.

It's going to be wonderful. You're going to be wonderful.

In the
LEAD-UP
to the
BIRTH

Many women are trained to nurture other people's needs, while men are often expected to focus elsewhere. It's not everyone's experience, nor is it necessarily inherent in our gender, but it's something we can be aware of and change.

For me, one of the hardest things about parenting is that I was trained to meet others' needs more than my partner was. So there are times when I'm noticing my child's needs *and* my partner's needs and I'm trying to fulfil them both, while mine have been lost somewhere behind the couch.

Take some time to think about your radar for seeing and meeting other people's needs.

Your partner's body is doing a huge, huge job right now. Even when pregnant bodies are asleep, they're working.

When you wake up in the morning, every morning, ask yourself what your partner's needs are – physical and emotional – before thinking about your own (not necessarily for the rest of your life, but for now). **DOES SHE NEED THE FIRST SHOWER, OR A LISTENING EAR, OR TO DANCE WITH YOU, OR SOME QUIET SPACE WHILE SHE DRINKS HER TEA?**

Do the same when you see her at the end of the day. Keep remembering to check in if there's anything she needs (without pestering her).

**THE THING IS, MEETING SOMEONE ELSE'S NEEDS IS
SUCH A GRATIFYINGLY GOOD FEELING.** If women do
it more, we don't do it only because we're oppressed
by the patriarchy (although that too); we do it because
it's next-level satisfying and the oxytocin hit is real.

Try practising emotional labour in other circumstances.
For example, once a day, during work or at a social
event, for one minute, think about each person in the
room – what do you think they need emotionally right
now? Can you offer anything that might fulfil it?

See if you can practise every day from now until the
baby is born.

Early parenthood is a good time to really enjoy meeting
other people's needs, so start developing your emotional
labour muscles now.

Also take time to think about what works for you in terms of regulating your emotions. How do you manage your big feelings?

IS IT DEEP BREATHING? A BIG LAUGH WITH A FRIEND? EXERCISE? SPACE TO CRY? Does particular music help? Or a moment looking out at the horizon?

Your partner will currently be getting a whole lot of information you're not. Other women will be sharing stories with her and giving her advice – it's part of the gendered nature of parenthood conversations.

Unless you're also being hit with daily incidental advice, you'll probably need to find some of that information yourself.

Consume some of the media aimed at mothers. Read books, check out websites. There is an internet of women sharing information about parenting.

Read a few stories about the mental load of parenting. (It's real. And much better shared.) What jobs already need doing? Buying a bassinet, car capsules, pram, baby clothes? Finding out about local child care, learning about safe sleeping? Make sure you're on the team, sharing all the thinking and research, as well as carrying out the tasks.

In the few months before the birth, get some one-on-one time with people you love who are parents.

Try to find as many different perspectives as you can, from people in various communities and backgrounds. Talk with people who gave birth and people who supported them.

ASK THEM IF THEY'RE COMFORTABLE TO TELL YOU THEIR BIRTH STORY. ASK THEM ABOUT THE FIRST FEW WEEKS OF THE BABY'S LIFE, AND ABOUT GOING BACK TO WORK. ASK HOW THEY FELT.

Be curious. Let them talk.

Ask some more.

Are there ways you can offer these friends support right now, emotionally and practically? By supporting them, you'll be learning more about what your own family's needs might be in the future.

At the same time, you'll be weaving yourself into the web of give and take that parent communities offer.

While getting ready for parenthood, how are you preparing to welcome your little one, *whoever they turn out to be?*

You're about to bring a small human into the world who may be part of, and interact with, any number of different communities. LGBTQIA+, disabled people and people of colour have done some deep and strategic thinking about parenting. It's worth seeking out and valuing these stories.

From the very beginning, the language you use, the attitudes you have, the faces and bodies your child sees and the picture books you share with them will shape their sense of self and their understanding of the world. Now is a good time to talk about this with your partner, before the baby's immediate physical needs take up all your attention. **WHAT WILL YOU DO SO YOUR CHILD KNOWS THEY *ALWAYS* HAVE A SAFE LANDING PLACE WITH YOU?**

If you're going to be the working parent, try to take as much time as you can off work. Take all your paid parental leave, if you're entitled to it, and then a little bit more if you can swing it. Everyone's situation is different, but if you possibly can, take six weeks and then see if you can negotiate a less-than-full-time load for a while.

It's an important time for supporting your partner – when my partner went back to work after six weeks, I was terrified – but also, it's an important time for your relationship with your baby.

This is the very beginning of your lives together. **THEY WILL GROW AND CHANGE VERY FAST IN THESE EARLY DAYS, AND ALL THE MOMENTS YOU CAN GET WITH THEM NOW WILL BE PRECIOUS.**

It's also a time to build confidence in all the skills you'll need on the days you're solo parenting.

Consider splitting contributions to your retirement pension with your partner, or contributing to her fund for a time. There should be information on how to do this online. Have a look at it now, because once the baby is born, form-filling is going to suck. Women generally retire with far less than men, which is partly the gender pay gap and partly because of the hit women take in their childbearing and caring years. Traditionally a woman's retirement plan has been her husband, and our financial structures haven't caught up with the times. So it's something you have to manage yourself.

Often, expectant parents focus so much on the birth that I wondered if it needed any more attention. But there are some things that are good to remember.

The first thing is, it's her body doing the birthing. She gets to make the decisions about how the birth goes.

Patriarchal structures around birth have historically devalued women's bodies and women's understanding of their own needs. Cultures are slow to change, and elements of this still affect birthing conditions, in particular for disabled and gender-diverse people and people of colour.

How can you be part of this team while supporting her and her choices? Ask her if there's anything she wants you to read or watch about the birth. Are there any classes she wants you to attend with her? Is there anything she wants to talk through?

Know her hopes and plans for the birth. **SHE NEEDS TO BE SURE THAT YOU ARE RIGHT BESIDE HER FOR THIS, THAT YOU WILL BACK HER UP AS SHE NAVIGATES WHAT MIGHT BE THE BIGGEST THING HER BODY HAS EVER DONE.**

Also, notice for yourself how you're going with this. Is there anything you're afraid of about labour and birth? What would you like to know about it? How are you feeling about the changes to your partner's body?

The actual development of a foetus is *incredible.*
TAKE SOME TIME FOR THE WONDER OF IT, THIS LITTLE UNBORN HUMAN WHO IS SOMEHOW YOURS.

Hospitals and birthing wards are full of wonderful, committed midwives, obstetricians and other healthcare experts who try hard to ensure that people who give birth can make their own powerful choices. Please listen to them.

But hospitals are also workplaces, with blanket policies, staffed by humans who need to finish shifts, who make mistakes and are embedded in a particular culture.

Birth can be deeply traumatic, both emotionally and physically. It can cause injuries that take months or even years to recover from. Procedures are sometimes carried out without the understanding or consent of the person giving birth.

While she's labouring, make sure your partner knows why any decisions are being made and what her options are. Ask the healthcare workers yourself. Does she have other choices?

If you possibly can, take the time to make sure you and the doctor still communicate with your partner. She may be loudly expressing her pain or seem non-verbal. You may feel panicky and afraid. Remember that doctors will be very clear if mother or baby are actually at imminent risk.

YOUR ROLE IN THIS IS TO BE HER ADVOCATE IN ALL THINGS. Trust her. Listen to her. It is her body at work.

YOU ARE STANDING AT THE EDGE OF SOMETHING TERRIFYING AND BEAUTIFUL. It's going to change your understanding of yourself, your relationship with your partner and your place in the world.

You're about to hold your baby in your arms. You're not alone. You can do this.

In the

FIRST
FEW
WEEKS

Often people say they fell in love with their baby as soon as they saw them – that big, overwhelming, life-changing feeling arrived in the very first moment.

Sometimes it doesn't happen like that. If it doesn't for you, or for your partner, that's okay. You're not broken. That's the other normal. Love also grows.

People can have all kinds of feelings after their baby is born and it's something for you to keep in mind and check in with your partner about.

In the first two weeks – even the first twelve weeks –
I was full of such big, raw, tender vulnerability.
There was a feeling of sacredness around the baby.
I wanted to take things very slowly. I didn't want
to have raucous toddlers in the house or listen to
Led Zeppelin. Catching the tram alone felt like an
enormous thing. The air felt rough. Noises felt harsh.
Part of me still wanted to be in a cocoon, and I wanted
everyone I met to treat me like I was precious.

I was on the brink of tears all the time – but they were
love tears. Always at the back of my throat, ready to
spill at the first sign of sweetness. I wish I had let
myself cry those tears more.

You will need to be sensitive and gentle. The feelings
may be so overwhelming that your partner won't know
what she needs. **HOW CAN YOU GIVE HER THE LOVE
AND SPACE SO SHE CAN FIGURE IT OUT AND TELL YOU?**

Your partner's body has literally laboured *for* you so you can have this child together. Now you can share in the labour of her recovery, mental and physical.

LET YOUR PARTNER TAKE CHARGE OF HER RECOVERY, BUT DON'T LEAVE HER ALONE WITH IT. You might book appointments or drive her there or walk the baby out the front of the clinic while she's inside. For those first two weeks I basically stayed in bed, except when I was on the couch, and I had a very untraumatic birth. So think about what your role will be, in the time when she needs to be in bed.

There's a whole lot of support around post-partum mental health. There are amazing women's health physios who know how to deal with pelvic floor issues and abdominal separation if your partner feels like that part of her recovery needs help.

Some of this recovery can feel shameful or as if treatment won't make a difference or is difficult to prioritise. In my experience it's so, so worth it.

The helplines available for mothers are also there for the people supporting mothers. Call them. Ask your questions.

If your partner is breastfeeding, she might find it easy. But she might find it fucking hard. Any difficulties can be heightened by feelings of guilt or failure, which are totally unwarranted but deeply felt. She will need much tender care from you. Listen. Be your sweet self with her.

Every time my baby latched on to feed, I had a sudden, desperate thirst reflex. This is really common. Get your partner a glass of water *every time* she starts breastfeeding. Don't even ask. Have straws in the house, so you can hold glasses up for her to drink while she holds the baby.

I was also *ravenous* when I was breastfeeding. Ten minutes late for dinner was a long wait. If dinner *was* late, nuts were good. **DINNER NOW IS BETTER THAN DINNER FANCY.**

In the first few weeks, baby-care and her own post-birth physical recovery should be your partner's *only* jobs. Unless she actively wants to do them for pleasure or a sense of identity, you should try to cover the rest: all the cooking, cleaning, laundry and organising of other humans.

But also, outsource the jobs that you can, so you can take moments to cuddle your family and to rest.

If you can, pay a cleaner for the first twelve weeks, or for the weeks immediately after you return to work. Talk with your partner about what domestic standards might slip for a while, when snuggling and bonding time are top priority. **PEOPLE WILL WANT TO DROP AROUND FOOD. THEY MAY OFFER TO WASH YOUR DISHES OR FOLD YOUR LAUNDRY. LET THEM.**

In those early stages, change most of the nappies (or diapers). Partly to give your partner a break from baby-care, but more because it's your chance to have intimate, connected time with the baby, to pay attention to their physicality, their face, the nuances of how they like to be spoken to, moved and held.

THIS IS YOUR CARE TIME, LIKE BATHING YOUR BABY AND SETTLING THEM TO SLEEP; BEING THE WARM BODY THEY REST ON. This is your chance to be together.

Do all you can to make sure your partner doesn't feel social obligations to anybody. When babies are born, especially first children, there can be a flurry of interest. Everyone wants to know all the details. Does she need you to take on the role of fielding all the phone calls and messages?

Be the visitor liaison so your partner doesn't have to manage the busy baby-cuddle calendar. Check how she's feeling about visit lengths and then send people home once they've reached her limit. That might be an hour. Or half an hour. Set them up so that it's only a short visit. Let them know you may actually need to call them on the day and postpone. If they've had a baby they should understand. If they haven't had a baby, tell them.

BE BRAVE ABOUT SETTING BOUNDARIES, EVEN IF YOU FEEL AWKWARD. Don't make your partner do that job today. Don't let her be nice to others at her own cost.

People are going to give the baby presents. Be the person who says thank you. **TAKE A CUTE PICTURE OF THE BABY WEARING THE CARDIGAN YOUR AUNTY KNITTED OR WAVING THE TOY FROM THEIR GRANDPARENTS.**

This is where you begin facilitating your child's relationship with their family and community. This is how you keep people connected.

Get right in the middle of your baby's healthcare. There are all kinds of little health hurdles a small human goes through, as well as bigger potential health complications. **THESE MIGHT FEEL SCARY, BUT THEY DON'T FOR A SECOND MEAN THAT YOUR BABY ISN'T WONDERFUL.**

Book the appointments, go to the maternal child health visits, be there for the vaccinations. If you're working and can use carer's leave, take it. You'll feel more empowered if you know your child's doctor. If you don't know them, it will be harder to jump in later when you're needed.

Doing all these jobs doesn't mean being stoic.
Take time to be soft. Appreciate your baby and your
partner. Lie down next to them. They're probably
very nice.

Breathe. Snuggle. Listen.

Sometimes men feel disconnected or less loved or less important when a baby comes along. As if the mother and the baby are everything and they are on the outer. If you're feeling that, know that it will pass. And it's not the truth.

THERE IS A PLACE FOR YOU, TO BE RIGHT IN THE MIDDLE, TO HAVE YOUR BIG GOOD HEART WIDE OPEN. To give and receive all the love.

In the

FIRST
THREE
MONTHS

(or so)

The early weeks and months of a baby's life can feel like forever when you're in them, but whatever you're experiencing will change. All the behaviours and habits of a little one shift constantly as they grow.

If it feels hard right now, I promise it will be different soon. And if it feels lovely, revel in it.

See if you can spend a little bit of time every single day focused only on your baby. Time when you are paying attention to them – not the jobs, not the news, not your phone.

It may only be three minutes. Or five. But do this every day: get yourself to their eye level or below, lie down or cuddle them on your lap if they're happy there, and then pay them quiet attention.

Let them lead. This time is not about you entertaining them. Notice what they are interested in, what they are saying, what they are asking you for. **NOTICE HOW GOOD THEY ARE AND HOW MUCH YOU LOVE THEM.**

The love time is what makes everything else doable. Soak it up.

Be rigorously fair with your spare time, if you have any at all. Keep asking yourself, **IS YOUR PARTNER GETTING TO EXERCISE, ENGAGE IN HER HOBBIES OR HAVE ANY TIME TO HERSELF?** Base decisions on your answer to that question. This newborn time will be over soon and hobbies and exercise become more possible.

Whenever you leave the house, come home on time. Five minutes late is a long, *long* five minutes.

I've heard mothers tell stories of walking to the bus stop so they can hand over their baby sooner once their partner returns from work. I've watched the clock with a sense of desperation, knowing I'm going to crack if the front door doesn't open soon. Come home on time.

MAKE SURE THERE'S ALWAYS FOOD IN THE HOUSE, particularly finger food that can be eaten one-handed, while holding or feeding the baby: snow peas, cherry tomatoes, cheesy polenta squares, bread that's already sliced, cheese that's already sliced, crackers, quiche in little squares, frittata in little squares, almonds, dried figs, bananas.

Sometimes people feel
'touched out' when they've
been holding a baby all day.
Touching their partner when
they finally have space is the
last thing they want.

Don't stop offering your
cuddles, but don't be
offended if she wants space.
**THE SIXTH LOVE LANGUAGE
IS DISTANCE. GIVE IT TIME.**

Sex after birth might be a big, big deal. It might take months and then need to be a very careful, slow, thoughtful thing. It might take a year or longer (it really might).

One gender stereotype in parenting is that dads are fun: they're funny, and tend to be the leaders of the physical play. If this is true for you, don't hold back. Children have a fierce need to play.

Do your best to make sure play time is not at your partner's expense or making her life harder. How can you include her in the play? Or not disturb her at all with the play? **HOW CAN YOU MAKE SURE EVERYONE IS FED AND THE HOUSE IS CLEAN, WHILE ALSO GETTING THE PLAYING IN?**

While you play, stay sensitive. Watch your baby's face and body language. Remember, laughter can sometimes be a response to shock and discomfort, rather than pleasure. What happens to your baby's face straight after the laughter? Lack of eye contact can be a baby's way of asking for a break.

Educate yourself about consent.

Consent starts with looking in a tiny baby's eyes and saying, 'I'm going to pick you up now.' And then giving them time to take in that information before you grab them.

CONSENT IS MAKING VERY SURE A LITTLE PERSON WANTS TO BE TICKLED BEFORE YOU TICKLE THEM, AND LISTENING WHEN THEY SAY STOP.

It's asking if they want a kiss or a cuddle and then paying attention to their body language. It's saying, 'How do you want to say goodbye to Grandma?' instead of 'Give Grandma a hug.'

Women often share their histories and fears about child safety and sexual assault with each other. We read the articles and think about how to keep our children safe.

Seek out some basic information on this early – as much to keep your child safe as to make sure your partner doesn't feel like she's the only one in your family thinking about it. Check if she wants to think about it with you. Be sensitive about when and where you have this conversation with her.

You're not going to get much sleep. It's probably going to be worse than you think and go on for longer than you imagine. The baby might wake up six times a night and be awake for an hour each time, and this might happen for months. How are you going to manage that between you?

DO WHAT WORKS FOR YOU TO BOTH GET AS MUCH SLEEP AS YOU CAN, WHILE BEING AS FAIR AS YOU CAN.

If you're bottle feeding this can look like taking it in turns during the night. If she's breastfeeding it might mean her heading to bed at 7.30 pm while you play with the baby until a 10 o'clock feed, or you taking the baby out for a big long walk from 5 am. It might mean you getting up after night feeds to change nappies and settle the baby while she goes straight back to sleep. It's going to depend on your bodies and how sleep works for each of you.

Remember that for a lot of people, working a paid job is not more tiring than staying home with a baby. Don't use work as an automatic excuse for one partner to get more sleep.

You're both going to feel exhausted and hopeless and sulky and furious. Your patience is going to be pushed like never before. And you are going to need to keep functioning through those feelings.

I'm not saying push them down or don't feel them or be a big man. I'm saying make sure there's dinner, on time, even if you feel really sooky. Find those moments for deep breaths or laughing or looking out to the horizon.

WHO DO YOU TALK WITH WHO HELPS YOU UNPACK AND CLARIFY WHAT'S SWIRLING AROUND IN YOUR MIND? Your partner may be so tired of meeting another person's needs that listening to you feels difficult right now.

Call a friend instead. Call your dad. Call another dad (one who will listen and won't blame your partner for your feelings). Call them and tell them how hard things are for two minutes, before you have to do the next thing.

Also, quick reminder, therapy is for *everyone*.

But talking with your partner might be good for her too; she might be wanting a big emotional connection with you. **SUPPORTING EACH OTHER IN YOUR MOMENTS OF FURY AND TIREDNESS, SHARING THE TIMES YOU BOTH FEEL LIKE YOU FUCKED UP, MIGHT BE JUST WHAT YOU BOTH NEED.**

Keep checking. Use your emotional labour radar. You've got this.

As they

GROW

UP

There are some things about parenting that are similar to the demands of a regular job. Bills need to be paid, emails need to be sent, things need to be bought and carried from one place to another. Logistics.

Remember, *if you don't do these jobs, your partner will have to*. Some of these jobs are about keeping your child alive and safe or obeying the law; they can't just be left undone. So do your share. Check if your partner feels like you're doing your share. **SOME JOBS MIGHT BE INVISIBLE UNTIL YOU'RE THE PERSON DOING THEM.**

At some point it might be worth making a list of all the jobs you're both thinking about and divvying them up between you. The more efficient you are as a team, the less total labour the two of you will be doing.

Actively take on your share of the thinking jobs (the mental load). **WHEN YOU SIGN UP FOR CHILD CARE OR SCHOOL MAKE SURE YOU'RE GETTING THE EMAILS TOO.** When the birthday party invites go out, use your number for the RSVPs. Be the guy who stocks the wrapping-paper stash.

Often men get credit in the workplace for being dads: fathers are viewed as more trustworthy, as good leaders. If you're doing a good job of parenting, people will adore that about you.

Meanwhile, early parenthood can be the time when women lose their career, when they are overlooked for positions or promotions because people see mothers as more committed to their children than to their work.

How can you support your partner to return to work in the way she wants to after her maternity leave? What does she need? Extend this thinking to your own workplace: how can you support the mothers you work with?

You might be driven to prioritise your paid work, possibly too much or too soon. Find corners to resist where you can.

Stretch out your morning cuddles. Save your emails for your paid hours. Leave your work on time. Your people are important too.

Hold your family. Do silly dancing in your lounge room. Rest. Care.

DO THIS WORK A LITTLE MORE AND THE OTHER WORK A LITTLE LESS.

Who stays home from work when your child is sick? Remember, someone working full-time has more paid leave. A day off for someone working part-time is a much greater portion of their working week.

Caring for a sick child is time to be close with them in a different way. **MAYBE STAYING HOME WITH YOUR LITTLE ONE IS A PRIVILEGE YOU'D LIKE TO HAVE?**

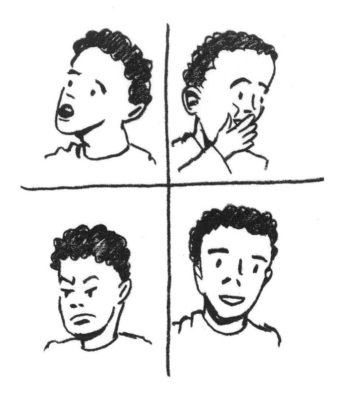

One of my favourite phrases about early childhood is 'behaviour is communication'. Your child may not be able to articulate how they are feeling but they will definitely be able to show you. Chances are they are not being 'naughty', they are trying to tell you how they feel.

HOW WILL YOU RESPOND TO THEIR BIG FEELINGS? HOW DO YOU THINK THEY MIGHT RESPOND TO YOURS? What you do now will impact how they communicate with you down the track.

You are going to be saying no to your child a *lot*. Toddlers will happily put themselves in the way of death every few minutes.

A busy road means nothing to a two-year-old. A four-year-old will eat enough sugar to make themselves vomit. Your job is to stop them, gently and firmly, over and over again, even though it makes them scream with anger or cry great sobs of grief. It's okay for children to be upset.

YOU CAN SAY NO KINDLY AND PERSISTENTLY, GOOFILY AND CREATIVELY. Have fun with it. Use a puppet hand. Use a robot voice. Get cheek to cheek with them and say it quietly with a kiss.

Get good at it. Practise. Can you stay kind and gentle after saying no to the same thing twenty times? Because that's your job. Every day. Things will run better if you're good at setting boundaries without succumbing to your own frustration.

Maintain your own friendships. Early parenthood can be a time when male friendships drop away, and relationships do change when you have children. Some of the ways we bond with our friends pre-children – late nights, alcohol and risk-taking adventures – will be much less available to you.

How can your friendships include your children? How can you stay close and have fun with your friends now you have so much else on your plate? How can you share times of ridiculousness and exhilaration, while your child is safe and right there beside you? Who can you be vulnerable with apart from your partner?

REACH FOR RELATIONSHIPS EVEN WHEN THEY FEEL TIRING OR TRICKY. This effort is a long-term investment in support structures for you and for your family.

Once your child is at school, the other parents nearby will be a massive help with afterschool care and those weeks and weeks of holidays.

Make friends with them. Make friends early. **THEY SAY IT TAKES A VILLAGE – BUT YOU PROBABLY DON'T LIVE IN A VILLAGE, SO YOU HAVE TO BUILD ONE.**

Don't leave your partner to make all the new friends. People who love your family will be supporting her and therefore you. How can you return that support? Ask your partner. Is she offering other families support that you can help with?

For generations women have checked in with each other at the school gates, swapped pick-up times, carpooled to ballet class. Now you get to be a part of this community. Jump in.

Champion all the activities once considered the mother's domain: facilitating close friendships by organising play dates; making sure your child feels comfortable and lovely in their clothes; checking to see that *everyone* is welcomed and included at the party.

THESE THINGS ARE NOT FRIVOLOUS OR SMALL. THEY MAKE LITTLE HEARTS BRAVE IN THE FACE OF THE BIG GRIEFS AND INJUSTICES LIFE HOLDS. They are the glue holding people together and they enable us to survive. This, too, is something you can give your child.

Now your partner is a mother, you need to know that Mother's Day is fucked. Someone I know called it a bullshit 'appeasement operation' and it seriously is.

Being a mother is so, so hard. Having one day a year when the world wants to give us fluffy pink slippers and a new Mixmaster is a pathetic attempt to make us feel better for the way sexism and motherhood hammer us every other day of the year.

Mother's Day is fucked, but do it anyway (unless your partner specifically asks you not to).

Give her all her favourite treats. **TELL HER WHAT YOU LOVE ABOUT THE WAYS SHE'S A MOTHER. TELL HER WHAT YOU LOVE ABOUT *HER*.** Tell her what you're grateful for.

Do these things the rest of the time, but really, *really* do them on Mother's Day.

The advertising around Father's Day is equally ridiculous. You may or may not be the kind of dad who wants power tools and whisky, but that's not what this day is really about. **IT'S A TIME TO NOTICE HOW MUCH YOU LOVE YOUR LITTLE ONE, AND HOW MUCH THEY LOVE YOU.**

Parenting takes up so much energy and can often be busy and logistics-oriented, so take this opportunity to notice what you're doing well. Do this every day, but really, *really* do it on Father's Day. However hard it may have been, you're here. You're a dad. You did it.

You might make mistakes and have moments of great guilt and shame. We all let our children down and it can feel awful.

Try not to be defensive when this happens. Admit your mistakes. Notice that you feel hot or cold or sick to the stomach. Breathe.

Society might not have trained you for this job, but you do have the capacity for it. Pick yourself up. How can you repair the damage? Try again. **STEP BACK INTO THE PLACE WHERE YOU LOVE AND ARE LOVED.**

Keep giving yourself moments every day when your child has your full attention and gets to be in charge. It might not be very long at all, but find that time to just be with them and let them lead while you love them.

Don't make it a boring, torturous thing, where you drag yourself into being a dinosaur *again* even though you hate that. Play is about both people wanting to be there.

Watch your child, listen to them, notice how gorgeous they are. Slow down your breath. **HOW MUCH DO YOU LOVE THEM?** Find the ways you both have fun together and feel connected.

Lastly

Thank you for reading these pages. I've been trying to imagine you, as you prepare for the tiny new life on the way. I hope there's something here that can make a difference as you step into being a dad. There may have been things that you disagreed with or that don't click for you right now, but that's okay and might change down the track. Pick out what resonates for you. You know your relationship best. Trust your judgement. Trust your partner. Trust your child as you walk the long path beside them into adulthood. However you do this, whatever decisions you make, remember you belong right here, in the warm heart of your family. Keep moving towards connection. You know how.

Acknowledgements

Thank you to my family. Jono, much of what we learned together is reflected here and I'm so grateful it's you I share the parenting with. Jack, something of your babyhood has made its way onto these pages and I obviously couldn't have written it without you. Pete and Chris, you continue to model being dads in beautiful, generous, caring ways. Jenny, you taught me to hold the kind of high expectations I write about here. Each of you made this book possible. I love you.

Several folks read early drafts and gave useful feedback and/or leant their words to this book. Thanks Anais Chevalier for the bullshit 'appeasement operation', Penni Russon for the 'internet of women', Jasper Peach for the 'safe landing place' and Lefa Singleton Norton for the thoughts on sharing the labour of recovery.

Special thanks to the team at Hardie Grant Books, especially Emma Schwartz, Emily Hart and Amy Daoud, who took a little letter and helped to make a book.

Finally massive, sky-high thank yous to Bernard, for that first walk in the park, your enthusiasm and for the pictures that bring all the love and life to this book.

Published in 2022 by Hardie Grant Books, an imprint of Hardie Grant Publishing

Hardie Grant Books (Melbourne)
Wurundjeri Country
Building 1, 658 Church Street
Richmond, Victoria 3121

Hardie Grant Books (London)
5th & 6th Floors
52-54 Southwark Street
London SE1 1UN

hardiegrantbooks.com

Hardie Grant acknowledges the Traditional Owners of the country on which we work,
the Wurundjeri people of the Kulin nation and the Gadigal people of the Eora nation,
and recognises their continuing connection to the land, waters and culture. We pay our
respects to their Elders past and present.

 A catalogue record for this
book is available from the
National Library of Australia

You'll Be a Wonderful Dad
ISBN 978 1 74379 848 5

10 9 8 7 6 5 4 3 2 1

Design by Amy Daoud
Printed in China by Leo Paper Products LTD.

 The paper this book is printed on is from FSC®-certified
forests and other sources. FSC® promotes environmentally
responsible, socially beneficial and economically viable
management of the world's forests.

AILSA WILD is an author, performer and creative facilitator. Her work includes collaborating with microbiologists to translate complex science into graphic novels and picture books. She has written two junior fiction series, Squishy Taylor and The Naughtiest Pixie, as well as one book for adults, *The Care Factor*. She lives in Melbourne with her partner and son and three little fishes.